Inspirational Signs for More Sunshine in Your Life

Volume I
A Book of Short Forms

Also by Carmen Micsa

Change Your Grip on Life Through Tennis!
A Player's Physical, Mental, Technical, &
Nutritional Guide for Improving Your Game

The PR – The Poetics of Running
A Book of Poetry in Motion

Morsels of Love
A Book of Poetry and Short Form

Holistic Journey Toward Wellness
A Collection of essays together with 21 authors

Inspirational Signs for More Sunshine in Your Life

Volume I
A Book of Short Forms

Carmen Micsa

Wistful Press
CARMICHAEL, CA

Copyright © 2023 by **Carmen Micsa**

All rights reserved. No part of this publication may be reproduced, distributed or transmitted in any form or by any means, without prior written permission.

Carmen Micsa/Wistful Press
8037 Fair Oaks Blvd., Suite 101
Carmichael, CA 95608
www.carmenmicsabooks.com

Book layout © 2023 BookDesignTemplates.com
Cover art by Carmen Micsa
Cover design by Heather Dunmoyer
Book formatting by Jenni Wiltz

Inspirational Signs for More Sunshine in Your Life – Volume 1 — 1st ed.
A Book of Short Forms
ISBN 978-0-9983097-6-7 (paperback)
ISBN 978-0-9983097-7-4 (eBook)

Dedications

For my husband **Catalin Micsa** and our sweet teenagers **Alex and Sophia**. They constantly bring sunshine into my life.

For my father **Danut Gramatic**, who was a watchmaker, which makes me the "daughter of time." He was also a great poet with a unique sensibility to the world around him.

For my mom **Cezarina Gramatic**, who visits us often and still travels around the world at 70. She should have her own inspirational sign with her favorite thing to say about getting her way in life: *"if I can't enter through the door, I will climb through the window."*

For my wonderful friend **Deirdre Fitzpatrick**, KCRA news morning anchor, who runs with me by the river whenever we both find the time. She inspired me to start writing on Medium, where I published many of these short forms collected in this book.

For my dear friend **Jenni Wiltz**, author of *The Red Road*, who has helped me with the formatting and publication of all my books. As she pointed out, I found inspiration in the mundane and brought you inspiration, joy, wonder, and laughter in things that we can easily overlook, such as the funny signs at the end of my street.

And last, but not least, for **Kurt Swanson**, owner of the Midas Auto Shop in Carmichael. His business signs, managed and changed weekly by one of his employees **Lisa Anderson**, are inspiring and make us smile.

Contents

Plan to Thrive in 2023	15
New Year's Resolutions — Make Them Good!	19
Life is Like Cotton Candy	23
The Texture of Joy	27
Go Ahead: Play it Cool!	31
Let Your Success Be the Noise	35
No Worries! Broccoli Doesn't Like You Either!	39
Big Foot Saw Me	43
Erasers	47
Coffee, Wine, or Both?	51
Are You a Good Mom or a Great Mom?	55
Let it Go, Let it Grow!	59
Open Doors	63
The Master and the Servant	67
Sharpen Your Ears, Get Rid of Your Fears	71
Cheesy Jokes That Make Us Smile	75
Make Your Own Joy	79

Chase Your Dreams	83
Is a Full Belly More Grateful?	87
Letting Others Be Kind to You	91
Light up the World with Kindness	95
Acknowledgments	97
About the Author	99

"When you actively notice new things, that puts you in the present…As you're noticing new things, it's engaging, and it turns out…it's literally, not just figuratively, enlivening."
– **Ellen J. Langer**

Enjoy every detail and magical moment in this book of short forms (stories that are only 150 words or less) inspired by the Midas Auto Repair sign at the end of my street in Carmichael, CA. Each short form will encourage you to listen better, notice extraordinary things in the ordinary moments, as well as make you smile, laugh, and maybe even take action to make small tweaks and changes in your lives.

All these morsels of love, patience, and attention to detail will delight you and everyone else in your lives. So, go ahead and purchase this book full of seeds of sunshine for all your loved ones. They deserve your gift of love and attention on a daily basis.

And, last but not least, plan to thrive in 2023 and beyond by exercising, eating healthily, reading more books, and listening to Seeds of Sunshine, a mother/daughter podcast that my daughter Sophia and I started in July 2022, on Apple Podcast, Spotify, or wherever you listen to podcasts!

Photo by Carmen Micsa, Hilo, HI

Plan to Thrive in 2023

Inspiring street sign

"Dreamers have ideas. Doers have plans: plan for a great new year!"

Street sign by the Midas Auto Repair in my neighborhood, Carmichael, CA

Dreaming is daring to reinvent yourself. Dreaming is also living a fictionalized life that can become ours with the right planning.

This sign made perfect sense to me after my recent interview on our *Seeds of Sunshine*, a mother/daughter podcast with Osnat Benari, leadership coach and author of *Starting from Scratch — Manage Change Like Your Career Depends on It*, who emphasizes the importance of starting from scratch with an actionable plan so that we can make the right changes to become successful. Benari also talks about adopting a learning mindset.

And last, but not least, never have a plan B. Make your plan A work.

Just thrive in 2023 and beyond!

Photo by Samanta Sokolova on Unsplash

New Year's Resolutions — Make Them Good!
Inspiring street sign

"Everything good has butter in it including resolutions!"

Street sign by the Midas Auto Repair in my neighborhood, Carmichael, CA

Interpreting quotes has become a passion of mine since high school when our Latin teacher asked us to write a 1,000-word essay analyzing a single quote. At first, that seemed impossible, but as I viewed the quote from multiple angles, I started to have fun writing about it, while my classmates muttered under their breaths about the monumental task.

The quote above is obviously funny and clever because when we make our resolutions palatable, we're more likely to stick to them. Like a buttery and delectable meal, resolutions give us something good and exciting to work towards.

However, we should make strong resolutions, not soft ones like melting butter.

Enjoy your butter in 2023! In moderation!

Photo by Yarden on Unsplash

Life is Like Cotton Candy

Inspiring street sign

> *"Life, like cotton candy, can be fluffy & sweet, sticky & messy."*

Street sign by the Midas Auto Repair in my neighborhood, Carmichael, CA

My father used to buy me swirls of pink love and laughter on a stick every time he took me to the fair.

As soon as my father handed me the pink cotton candy I squealed and clapped my hands in anticipation of the sugar rush to follow. The fluffy and sweet cotton candy stuck to my face, lips, and fingers like super glue.

My father laughed and kissed my messy cheeks. He loved to see my green eyes dance with joy, as he recounted these sweet and sticky moments later on when I was older.

As for me, I remember my father's serene blue eyes particularly on January 29th, his birthday.

He would have turned 78.

Photo by Kevin Fitzgerald on Unsplash

The Texture of Joy

Inspiring street sign

*"Joy has a texture &
you can feel it in your heart."*

Street sign by the Midas Auto Repair in my neighborhood, Carmichael, CA

When I think of the texture of joy, I imagine a red velvet dress. When I feel the lush velvet, my fingers get ticklish at first, after which I get in touch with all the deep emotions inside my heart.

The joy of living, laughing, and merely breathing is a texture that slips on my being in waves of silk and cotton, but mainly velvet.

Feeling joy's texture requires the faith of a blind man who moves around relying on sounds and memories.

And when sunshine refuses to crack open the darkness, remember that joy can be felt within our hearts.

Photo by Alexander Krivitskiy on Unsplash

Go Ahead: Play it Cool!

Funny street sign

---

*"I don't have gray hair.
That's just wisdom highlights!"*

Street sign by the Midas Auto Repair in my neighborhood, Carmichael, CA

These neighborhood signs provide entertainment and get my creative juices flowing, highlighting the grayness, or the greatness of this story depending on your perspective.

When I first discovered my first white hair in my mid-40s, I plucked it with alacrity for fear that this gray matter could quickly spread around to my light brown hair. I thought that

I could efface this abnormal appearance and be done.

Soon a few more gray hairs appeared. I plucked them out faster than a gardener could remove an invasive plant.

Yet, when the wisdom hairs kept popping up more frequently, I just played it cool, and hope you will, too.

Photo by Nghia Le on Unsplash

Let Your Success Be the Noise
Inspiring street sign

"Work hard in silence. Let your success be the noise."

Street sign by the Midas Auto Repair in my neighborhood, Carmichael, CA

When I first read this inspiring message, I immediately thought of my father who had lived his life quietly — only to raise his head with pride upon achieving true success. I thought that my father never bragged about me to his family and friends, but I found out later that he did.

To my wise father, success was not merely a snowball, but an avalanche.

Working in silence was second nature to my father, who was a watchmaker dusting the hands of time. I work quietly, too, but I share what I am doing with close friends, and even trumpet it on social media.

I look forward to success being my noise, and I hope you will, too!

Photo by Hayes Potter on Unsplash

No Worries! Broccoli Doesn't Like You Either!
Funny street sign

The funny sign at the end of my street reminded me of our son Alex when he was little.

I used to chase him down the kitchen with a broccoli stalk in my hand, hoping that he ate it and even liked it.

Sigh! Wishful thinking!

I really wanted Alex to eat more vegetables, but he was a picky and fussy eater. I was at a loss until one day I read a great article in *The Parenting Magazine* about enticing kids to eat more veggies.

The sneaky way to make kids love broccoli?

Just sprinkle grated Parmesan cheese on top and pretend that the broccoli stalks/trees are covered in snow. Make a game out of it!

And it worked for a little while, but now, our teenage son is convinced that broccoli doesn't like him either.

Photo by Matthew McCarthy on Unsplash

Big Foot Saw Me
Funny street sign

"Big Foot saw me yesterday, but no one believed him."

Street sign by the Midas Auto Repair in my neighborhood, Carmichael, CA

Most of you know that funny, quirky, and wise street signs, as well as license plate messages, tickle my funny bone.

Finding cool signs as I drive around and writing about them is similar to my eagerness to break a fortune cookie into a million pieces to extract the message inside. The joy of seeing new signs and deciding whether the message is good enough for me to write about is like panning for gold.

The humor or wisdom that pops up at me while I drive around town makes me smile, reflect, and memorize the lines to sprinkle them during my runs with friends.

But wait till I mention Big Foot during my next run!

Photo by Carmen Micsa, Midas auto repair sign, Carmichael, CA

Erasers

Wisdom street sign – prose poem

To make a mark in the world, one needs a good eraser to eradicate mistakes, misfortunes, and miscommunications.

I remember how proud I was of the white eraser that smoothed out time's wrinkles for me in one swift swoosh across the lined notebooks. The pink erasers smelled like bubble gum but smeared and blurred my mark on the world. I avoided them while looking for ways to beautify my work the same way a gardener adds colorful flowers next to their vegetables. I was also discreet with my eraser, for some of our teachers reminded us that erasers are nothing but the fool's tool — temporarily making us look cool.

Stay away from erasers!

Photo by Carmen Micsa, Midas auto repair sign, Carmichael, CA

Coffee, Wine, or Both?

Funny street sign

Although I'm not a coffee drinker, I grew up in Romania, where coffee replaced the boring glass of water at all hours of the day. When visiting friends and relatives, coffee was the starting point in any conversation, as well as the liquid sunshine that everyone was in dire need of.

Seeing this sign, I smiled and saw coffee as a seed of change in perspective, demeanor, and even outlook on life.

Add to this a glass of wine for the things that we cannot change and we're on the path of changing ourselves when we're unable to change a situation, as Viktor Frankl said.

So, what's for you? Coffee, wine, or both?

Photo by Annie Spratt on Unsplash

Are You a Good Mom or a Great Mom?

Funny street sign

"Good moms let u lick the beaters. Great moms turn them off first."

Street sign by the Midas Auto Repair in my neighborhood, Carmichael, CA

My memories about licking the beaters revolve around my mom's delicious strawberry souffle that she made every summer. My father usually bought them from the market and would proudly display them on our kitchen table.

Recipe:

Two cups of diced ripe strawberries
4 egg whites only
1 cup of sugar

Use the mixer to beat the egg whites and slowly fold in the sugar till the eggs turn foamy and stiff. After that add the strawberries and mix them well. Remove the beaters dripping with pink sweetness of warm strawberry souffle and pass them to your kids, dogs, cats, you name it.

And if you're wondering, my mom always turned the beaters off.

Photo by Darius Bashar on Unsplash

Let it Go, Let it Grow!
Inspiring street sign

> *"Let some things go, and let other things grow."*

Street sign by the Midas Auto Repair in my neighborhood, Carmichael, CA

When I was 14 years old, I went to boarding school in Timisoara to study English about 33 miles from my hometown Lugoj, Romania.

I used to take the train. One of my favorite things to do was looking inside each compartment as if it were a separate movie with a new and exciting cast of actors.

The trains were rather unclean — smelling of stinky socks and cigarette smoke. The stench of sweaty armpits was nauseating in the summer heat, but I trained myself to let those things go, while chatting with many interesting travelers and learning new things.

We can all learn to grow by letting go!

Photo by Vadim Babenko on Unsplash

Open Doors
Inspiring street sign

"When life shuts a door, open it again. It's a door. It's how they work."

Street sign by the Midas Auto Repair in my neighborhood, Carmichael, CA

The Midas auto shop in my neighborhood attracts attention by posting wise and funny signs in front of their building.

This quote made me smile and think of my mom who is relentless when she wants something. Her favorite thing to say is: "*If I can't enter through the door, I will climb through the window.*"

As you can tell, my mom is quite determined and stubborn when pursuing a goal. I also inherited this trait from her, which serves me well in my real estate business, writing, and marathon running.

Trust me on this: life is full of open doors!

Photo by Andrew S on Unsplash

The Master and the Servant
Funny street sign

"Dogs have owners. Cats have staff."

Street sign by the Midas Auto Repair in my neighborhood, Carmichael, CA

Our family loves dogs, although I have never owned a dog because I grew up in an apartment back in Romania. My mom repeated that I couldn't have pets, although my dad seemed ready to buy me a dog.

Now as a grown-up, my husband says no dog, as that would mean having a third child.

However, if we were to have another pet besides our sweet Peter bunny, we would definitely feel better being a master than a servant to a cat. I like cats, too, but I sense their haughtiness even when they snuggle and rub against my legs, whereas dogs let me know through a submissive look that I am the master.

So, who are you? The master or the servant?

Photo by saeed karimi on Unsplash

Sharpen Your Ears, Get Rid of Your Fears
Inspiring street sign

"Quality of life begins between your ears."

Street sign by the Midas Auto Repair in my neighborhood, Carmichael, CA

This is the type of quote that makes me pause and think because it says: hear me out!

Listening is one of those rare qualities that few people possess anymore. It is the holy grail that brings us closer to God and mankind.

While I can't say that I am the greatest listener, I work hard to hone my listening skills, polishing them every day, as if knives that can be easily sharpened by the right tool.

And maybe that's all it takes to become a better listener: a sharpener that can simply work its magic and transform our ears into funnels of retained information, emotions, and fears.

Go ahead: get rid of your fears and sharpen your ears!

Photo by Austin Lowman on Unsplash

Cheesy Jokes That Make Us Smile

Funny street sign

"Tell me a flat tire joke. No pressure!"

Street sign by the Midas Auto Repair in my neighborhood, Carmichael, CA

Our neighborhood Auto repair shop sure makes us smile.

There is something about cheesy jokes that we all seem to gravitate towards. I even use them in our *Seeds of Sunshine, a mother/daughter multigenerational podcast* at the beginning of each episode. All my guests seem to genuinely enjoy them.

Or maybe they fake laughter…

However, I think our guests love to laugh. My cheesy jokes simply break the ice and make us more comfortable with each other.

To give you a little more context, I was born and grew up in communist Romania for 16 years, and jokes were the saving rope that we threw at each other to brighten up our lives.

Smiles for happier lives!

Photo by Nuria Duran, American River, Sacramento, CA

Make Your Own Joy

Inspiring street sign

---

*"Life won't throw you parties.
You gotta make your own."*

Street sign by the Midas Auto Repair in my neighborhood, Carmichael, CA

Making our own parties? That doesn't seem fun, right?

We typically love to get invited to parties and partake in joy together with others, but oftentimes we need to throw our own parties to celebrate small daily victories, such as being punctual, exercising, getting things checked off our to-do lists, meditating, resting, eating healthy, etc.

These parties don't necessarily need music or noise, but a celebratory attitude is highly encouraged. Moreover, when we throw our own parties, we remind ourselves how good it feels to achieve greatness. We pat ourselves on the back. We acknowledge that our lives are staged and orchestrated parties.

So, go ahead: dance as if no one is watching! Throw that party on!

Photo by Carmen Micsa, Cronan Ranch Trails, CA

Chase Your Dreams

Inspiring street sign

"Chase your dreams because your dreams won't chase you."

Street sign by the Midas Auto Repair in my neighborhood, Carmichael, CA

I have always dreamed of becoming a published author and was determined to chase my dreams ever since I started to write around nine years old.

Dreams are like clouds resting on top of mountains. Pillows of hope.

We see the clouds float around high in the sky and feel defeated by the distance and chasm created. Yet, once we decide to chase our dreams, they get closer and more tangible. They become part of our life story.

In my case, the more I wrote and published my work, the closer I was to chasing and achieving my dreams. No longer intimidated.

What are you waiting for? Get busy chasing what and who you treasure in life.

Photo by Carmen Micsa, Thanksgiving dinner, 2022

Is a Full Belly More Grateful?

Funny street sign

"It's Thanksgiving! Don't forget to set your scale back to 10 lbs."

Street sign by the Midas Auto Repair in my neighborhood, Carmichael, CA

Holidays are not only a time to get together with the people we love, but also ways to express our love of food and through food.

It is only my family and my mother here in America, so our holidays are a combination of traditional Romanian foods, such as bouef salad, or what Americans would call potato salad, and American ones.

To me, Thanksgiving would not be the same without oven-roasted turkey and the sweet and sour orange cranberry sauce that I buy fresh from Trader Joe's. The variety of our dishes might mean that we have more grateful bellies.

Ideally, not 10 pounds heavier.

Photo by Debby Hudson on Unsplash

Letting Others Be Kind to You
Inspiring street sign

> *"Let others be kind to you.*
> *Light the world."*

Street sign by the Midas Auto Repair in my neighborhood, Carmichael, CA

With Christmas around the corner, we're buzzing with excitement, buying presents for our loved ones and making everyone happy.

But do you ever stop to take care of yourself to alleviate the compounding stress that the holidays inevitably bring into our lives? How about letting others be kind to you and light up your world?

Whenever you feel that you are not doing enough for others, take a short break and allow a loved one, a friend, or a stranger be kind to you.

And if letting others be kind to you is not something that you consciously seek out, why not change roles this holiday season?

It will make you kinder and more loving!

Photo by Carmen Micsa, Christmas trees at Carmichael Park, CA

Light up the World with Kindness

Inspiring street sign

*"Compliment your neighbor —
Light up the world."*

Street sign by the Midas Auto Repair in my neighborhood, Carmichael, CA

Carmichael Park, where my husband and I play tennis, lights up our world with their real tree and the artificial one every December.

Although we never want to extend a fake compliment, one thing is certain: no small or big compliment will go unnoticed. When we sincerely compliment family, friends, or perfect strangers, their faces lit up brighter than all 82 feet of the Rockefeller Christmas tree.

As we notice their inner joy blink at us, that's when we feel more inclined to keep passing back the kindness baton to others.

A compliment is noticing the light in others and pointing it out.

Go ahead: light up the world with kindness! What a great FREE and generous Christmas gift!

Acknowledgments

A million thanks to the following who have shaped this book and have helped me over the years become the writer/poet I am today: Jenni Wiltz, my Sac State classmate, friend, and brilliant writer, who has helped me with all the publishing and formatting process of this book and my other two books, Doug Rice, my most inspiring creative writing professor and acclaimed author, Sheree Meyer, the Chair of the Sacramento State University English Department when I got admitted into the English program, and last, but not least, Joe and Gay Haldeman, my wonderful and most supportive friends, who brought us to America. Haldeman is the winner of both the Nebula and Hugo Awards for his science fiction novels.

Special acknowledgments to *The Daily Cuppa* Medium publication, where many of these short forms have been published.

About the Author

Born and raised in Romania, Carmen Micsa moved to America in 1995, where she and her future husband Catalin Micsa have made Sacramento their home. Carmen Micsa has earned BA and MA degrees in English (Creative Writing) both from Sacramento State University. She has published her first book *Change Your Grip on Life Through Tennis* in 2016. She also published articles in a few local and national publications and a memoir piece *Grandpa's Garden* in the anthology *From Sac Home Myths & Other Untruths* together with some of her graduate school classmates.

In 2020, Micsa published her first poetry book *The PR – The Poetics of Running, A Book of Poetry in Motion*. It was her pandemic project that kept her sane and motivated to write and publish.

In 2021, Micsa published her second poetry book *Morsels of Love, A Book of Poetry and Short Form*.

In 2022, Micsa published the anthology *Holistic Journey Towards Wellness* with 20 other authors with essays on positivity, health, fitness, and cooking.

Besides writing, Micsa enjoys being a mother to her two beautiful and kind children Alex and Sophia. She is also the broker/CEO/founder of her real estate company, Dynamic Real Estate, Inc., and prides herself for being organized and efficient in leading a balanced life.

Micsa is an avid runner, who has completed 16 marathons, including London, Boston, New York City, Chicago, Berlin, and Tokyo.

Besides running, Carmen loves to play tennis and pickleball with her husband and her two teenage children Alex and Sophia. She also likes to swim, bike, and practice Pilates.

For more info on her books, please visit Carmen Micsa's website at www.carmenmicsabooks.com and her blog, www.runningforrealestate.com.

www.ingramcontent.com/pod-product-compliance
Lightning Source LLC
Chambersburg PA
CBHW070435010526
44118CB00014B/2059